Babushka's View

Barbara James
Babushka's View

Babushka's View
ISBN 978 1 76041 555 6
Copyright © text Barbara James 2018

First published 2018 by
GINNINDERRA PRESS
PO Box 3461 Port Adelaide 5015 Australia
www.ginninderrapress.com.au

Contents

1	The Room With the View	7
2	It Begins – Dad	12
	Pirate	13
	I Really Miss You Then	14
3	Judgement – Mum	17
	To Your Only Daughter…Mum	19
	It All Happened In Finlayson Street	21
4	Nana	24
5	Down The Cape	28
6	Brother	31
7	Escape – Music and Uni	37
	White Fedora	38
8	Schooldays	45
	Primary Days	46
9	From Aldgate Valley To St Kitts	51
10	Lost	57
	Thank You	58
	Funeral	60
11	Dealing With Damage	63
	Migraine	64
12	The Other M Word	70
	A Testing Time	70
13	Active Witness	75
	This Little Cup	76

'The unexamined life is not worth living' – Socrates

1
The Room With the View

It is always there. I can count on the view to never let me down, never judge. Always the same yet forever changing; the river, bright blue to green to grey by day, only dressing in formal black at night. The sky, arm in arm with the wind and clouds yet forever at their mercy, is my daily tonic. The sky sings of freedom, hope and possibilities, telling me that even chaos can be followed by calm.

Sydney has given me a new start, a new life, a room with a view. The move from the familiar to the unknown was scary but necessary. I love Adelaide but she was suffocating me with her memories, dry heat and ghosts. This was the only way to stop the relentless presence of those ghosts, to pack myself up with my few treasures and move away, let them go. Places have always held great significance to me; I feel places. I needed them to help bring memories back. Perhaps I no longer need those memories in my life. Now that I have left those places, the ghosts have retreated. Now I can recall the past if and when I choose, rather than it threatening to engulf me.

None of the shine has gone since I moved to Sydney. This place so full of challenge and vibrant beauty.

I feel that I am seeing this new world through my eyes and not through the filter of others. I am in control of my life; I give myself permission to be selfish. I feel a pang of guilt for writing these words. This is a new feeling; I have always been propelled by duty. Don't get me wrong, I have embraced this role with relish, but the rewards came from others; now they come from me. I find myself grinning, silently congratulating myself, setting my own challenges and constantly surprising myself. And I set the pace.

Was it karma or just good luck that I found myself an unassuming yet perfect apartment in beautiful Hunters Hill with the sleepy Lane Cove River on one side and the bustling Parramatta on the other? I had never lived near water and now here I was between two rivers which meet at Woolwich to join the magnificent Harbour. At any time, day or night, I have the view; I can look forward, I can breathe again.

When I first arrived, when everything was new, I attempted adventures daily. I began to feel self-propelled without the dark overhang of dread and the weight of responsibility. I relished the anonymity, becoming a bemused, somewhat detached, observer of this new life around me. Choosing not to drive, I quickly became queen of the ferry and happy to ride the buses. Not driving was liberating. I had hated it even in Adelaide; being trapped alone inside a fast-moving, potentially lethal machine spelt danger, if not torture, for me. I had made a promise to myself when I made the move, to eliminate as much stress as possible from my life. Besides, you get to interact with your surroundings when you hand over the responsibility of getting from A to B to someone else. As Gloria Steinem says, 'I don't drive, because adventure starts the moment I leave my door.'

My regular haunts in pursuit of adventure became Circular Quay, the Harbour, Cockatoo Island, the MCA, Dendy Cinema, the State Library and the Art Gallery, all exquisitely beautiful. Closer to home there was my village, my river and my walks. Gorgeous Turner clouds from sunrise to sunset, the climate mild. Summer is blue sky, warm, moist air, day and night, not like being inside a fan-forced oven. Winter is sunny but fresh, not arctic, while spectacular thunderstorms announce the subtropical wet. I have birds all around me; I hear their songs and cries wherever I go. Magpies, currawongs, crows, kookaburras, cockatoos, lorikeets, crested pigeons, and of course the ubiquitous noisy miners and 'devil birds'. I tamed a pair of magpies who were constant companions for a while until they sadly moved away. I would love to tame a currawong; they look so proud and fierce, but are sadly so timid. One black prince, with his red monocle, sits on my balcony sometimes, but that's his limit for now.

The beauty around me, like the coffee, is everywhere. And the

Harbour. I don't think I shall ever tire of its magnificence. It is so easy to visualise the early days of Sydney Town, in the thick walls and narrow lanes, the golden sandstone mansions and the tiny cottages. Or imagine the grime and the stench coming from neighbourhoods which now fetch millions of dollars. And the art, the theatre and music, like the coffee, is everywhere, and much of it is world-class.

I am engaged in an enduring love affair with the ferries: they are calm, relaxing and unthreatening, the antithesis of driving a car. I always feel special when riding the ferry, like a kid getting a treat.

I love to walk here. There is always something new to see and when you look, you can see into the distance. Because this city is anything but flat, there is always a view. Hills, coves, rivers, bays, bridges and the sky, the ever-changing sky. Here I feel safe, mostly invisible. It is as though I had fled South Australia to invent a new self. I am learning to look outwards, to the view, rather than inwards, to the past.

I found myself becoming acutely aware of other people but from a distance, almost voyeuristic. You can do that when you're invisible; it happens to women of a certain age and I quite like it.

It was early evening, warm and perfect. I had become accustomed to taking a photo of the same view at the same time, dusk, on consecutive days. My view of choice was across the water to the city and the Bridge from the wooden seat at Woolwich Wharf. Once I had frozen the moment in a photo, I began reading.

The wharf was quiet. A ferry had just left. My book demanded a certain amount of attention; it was outlining the history of philosophy and I had come to the section on Kant. I was just starting to get my head around his concept of morality when a young man, obviously flustered, interrupted me. In less than perfect English, he asked me to confirm his whereabouts. I assured him he was definitely at the Woolwich Wharf. I returned to Kant. The young man, even more flustered, tried to explain that he was supposed to meet someone there but they hadn't arrived, or at least that's what I supposed he was trying to tell me. I again tried to reassure him and returned to Kant, albeit with difficulty.

His stress level increasing, he implored me to use his mobile phone to call this invisible person to explain the situation. I was then faced with a philosophical dilemma: what do I do? Do I help him, do I have some sort of moral duty?

My thoughts went like this. How can I explain a situation I don't fully understand myself? I feel uncomfortable using a stranger's phone. For that matter, I feel uncomfortable talking to this stranger let alone another. It is nearing sunset, I am a woman on my own. Will he grab me, will he steal my bag, what does he really want from me?

After a few tortured seconds, I made my decision. 'No, sorry, I can't make the call.'

The poor young man, still looking anguished, retreated.

I closed my book and walked away.

Later I reflect, with some moral anguish, do I attract needy people, did I make the right decision, what would Kant have done?

A week later, again at dusk and in this same spirit of adventure, I headed to the same seat at the wharf and took my photo of the same view across the water. Even though hazy, it was still warm and beautiful.

The wharf again was deserted. I was still reading my philosophy book, intent on finishing so I could return it to a friend. My head was deep in the challenges of existentialism when I became aware of a young man nearby, just in my line of vision. I guessed he was in his early twenties. He appeared agitated but also strangely calm. There seemed to be a problem with his shoes; he was taking them off, choosing to go barefoot. I realised then we were not alone; he was talking softly to an older woman in an idling car, trying to reassure her that he was OK but for his shoes. I could sense something was wrong. The young man by then was moving around quite close to me, which made me a little uncomfortable even though he wasn't saying or doing anything to me. I tried to concentrate on Camus.

It became clear that the older woman was his mother and that she was clearly concerned for him. His movements became more and more erratic; he was taking his shoes off then putting them back on, all the while assuring his mother he would be OK, with which she did not agree. At no stage were voices raised.

Feeling increasingly uncomfortable yet unable to stop watching, I moved away to a seat in the park opposite and tried to continue to read. After some moments, the mother got out of her car, motor still running, and tried to reason with her son. I could not hear the words, only snatches.

'Mum, I'll be fine. Broken shoes. Mum, what are you doing?'

Words were not necessary; it was clear she did not want her son to take the ferry, but she was not raising her voice. She got in and out of her car several times, finally grabbing his bag from him and hurling it into the boot. He came close to getting in the car but decided against it. Suddenly she gave up, taking off in her car, accelerating hard, running right over his discarded shoes and disappearing at speed up the hill. He, barefoot, no bag, quietly sauntered down the ramp to the wharf into the approaching evening.

I drove home, surprisingly affected by the scene I had witnessed. I could not get the young man and his mother out of my head. I worried for them both long into the night. Would he be all right, was he having an 'episode', would he be attacked, taken advantage of or worse, would he drown or otherwise harm himself? And the mother: I could feel her worry, her agitation, her resignation. How many times had she gone through this before? I knew she would do it all again.

Is it dusk that brings out strangeness in people? 'Between a wolf and a dog,' as Georgia Blain describes this indeterminate time; not day, not night.

Do I attract tension, worry, drama? I wonder what the existentialists would have to say about this. According to Sartre, we decide what we perceive in the world by selecting what is significant for us. To exist is to create your own life. Do I then select these things to focus on and do they in turn help to determine who I am?

2
It Begins – Dad

It was 1951, the war was over, Australia was beginning to prosper. I was one of many baby boomers.

I arrived into the world with no drama – Mum healthy and happy to be moving into her own home away from her parents, Dad proud that he had created their dream home himself. He made the bricks and carried building materials on the handles of his pushbike while Mum nailed the floorboards while pregnant with me. New life, new hopes and dreams.

Dad drove Mum to the hospital in his beloved Oldsmobile and I set about becoming a particularly chubby baby, awash with a never-ending supply of milk from Mum's gigantic breasts.

My early years were happy. I grew and played at will, enjoying the freedom of the House That Dad Built. I had my own bedroom with books, dolls and Annie Oakley costume. My backyard was a wonderland filled with flowers, shrubs, birds, fruit trees and Dad's orchids. I even had a pet hen called Sally. There were birthday parties, piano and ballet lessons and I was even a regular on a TV show on Channel Nine called *Southern Stars*, a bit like *Young Talent Time*. It was there I gained confidence and a love of performance (skills which came in handy when I became a teacher later in life).

I was fortunate to have the most wonderful father, whom I adored. Having received only a basic school education did not limit Dad, who went on to be a consummate storyteller, builder, worker in metal, canvas and wood, orchid grower and mechanic. He was utterly selfless, funny and fair. He loved me unconditionally and I cannot remember him ever getting angry with me. This sentence makes me pause. How lucky was I? He laid a wonderful foundation but was a hard act to follow, as I discovered later when experimenting with my own relationships.

Caring for a disabled son and an emotionally and financially dependent wife while running a small canvas business must have been challenging. However, he was able to put me through years of ballet and piano classes and support me through school and university. And all this with sight in only one eye, having been blinded in the other in a work accident. From him, I learned persistence and patience but, above all, selflessness.

In the following two poems, I try to express the depth of my love for him and the closeness between us:

Pirate

I would sit waiting
In the green Holden ute
Loving the smell
Of the canvas
Tipping the wooden spirit level
Back
And forth
Waiting for dad
To finish his quote

What's a quote?
I'd ask

I measure
I quote the price
I make the blind
Then I nail it to the window

So that's why you're blind
Dad?

Dad looks at me
With his one good eye
The other milky white

Yeah,
Copped a piece of steel
Flew right in my eye
Hardly felt it
But it stayed there
Rusting
Till the doctors
Took it out
And my sight with it

I learnt never to
Jump out at dad
Or play tricks
On his blind side

I didn't mind
I had my own real
Pirate

I Really Miss You Then

Xmas Day, Dad
I really miss you then
Your plum pudding
Boiling in its cloth skin
Heaving with fruit
Drunk with brandy
'Who's got the threepence?'
    I'd hope it was me

Guy Fawkes's Day
November the 5th
'Gunpowder, treason and plot'
Your birthday, Dad

You'd struggle through the door
Arms laden with brown paper bags
'What d'ya get, what d'ya get?'
I'd say
Knowing there'd be
    Cartwheels
    Rockets
    Threepenny bungers
And the promise of colour and noise

We'd dance around the Guy
Flames leaping
My face lit up with colour
How I still love the fireworks
And how I miss you then

Sunday mornings, Dad
You'd sit out the back
In the sun
Pretending to be asleep
While I'd comb your hair
Thick, dark and wavy
Like mine
And I'd decorate it with flowers
I can still feel the warmth
Of those mornings
With you

Cape Jervis jetty
Sitting close
You and me, Dad
Struggling with the wind

And the cold
Dark chocolate for energy
And a thermos of tea
Mixed with the squid ink
And tommy ruff scales

Few words would pass between us
But words were unnecessary
I was in heaven
And now
I miss you
Still

Where did those many selfless acts of generosity and kindness come from? I know he had fond memories of his father too, who died when Dad was still a young boy.

Knowing I was a mad Beatles fan, he would bring home, grinning from ear to ear, their latest 45rpm record as soon as it was released. I didn't know of any other fathers who did something like that. I knew he was special.

One night, aged about sixteen, I came home late and very drunk, having spent the evening with friends drinking port from a flagon while toasting marshmallows and sausages over a makeshift fire in the foothills. I crept into my room, collapsed into bed and immediately threw up. Too drunk to care, I just rolled over and sank into a heavy sleep and into the warm vomit.

The next morning, instead of berating me for my behaviour, as my mother certainly did, my dad simply came gently into my room, surveyed the rather disgusting scene and said with a twinkle in his eye, 'Well, you'd better stay clear of red wine.'

And I did.

3
Judgement – Mum

My mother was vivacious, attractive and talented. She had a magnificent singing voice and a captivating smile. From her, I got my sense of style, my love of music and the arts, ballet in particular, and my gardening green thumb. How I wish things had been different for her.

She was one of many women of her generation, born just after World War I, before girls were valued equally in either family or society. I know little about her education, only that she attended the local primary school in Adelaide. She raised two children but never learnt to drive a car, never worked outside the home and rarely went out unaccompanied by my father. I suppose she could be described as a typical 1950s housewife, stuck in a comfortable yet limited home setting.

She had grown up in a family where the boys all received a good education and went on to become professionals – a solicitor and two accountants – while she and her sister left school early and became stay-at-home wives and mothers. Her parents were comfortable financially and owned a large bungalow in one of Adelaide's well-established, leafy suburbs. The boys were encouraged to pursue their interests, which included target rifle shooting and photography. One of the boys served with the RAAF in New Guinea.

My mother was blessed with a beautiful soprano voice and as a young girl had asked her father for singing lessons so she could pursue her talent. This was denied, even though there was always plenty of money for the boys. I believe she could have become an opera singer if she had been given the training and opportunity. Having seen examples of the meticulous sketches and beautiful embroidery she produced before she got married, I believe she had a talent for the visual arts as well. I feel sad that she was never given the chance to develop all that artistic potential.

The closest she came to self-expression was in creating a never-ending array of sweet, flummery cakes, slices and tarts to take to morning or afternoon tea. She always seemed to be trying to prove she was better than the other women; it was always a competition. I realise now she was just trying to create an identity, and how important it must have been to her to maintain it. Like so many other women in her situation at that time, she was undoubtedly unfulfilled and frustrated but conditioned by society to expect nothing more.

Photographs of her as a young unmarried woman show her as outgoing, attractive and ready for fun. My memories of my mother reflect a woman with two faces. The face she showed to the world was the happy, carefree, fun-loving face of her youth. Behind that face was a stew of anxiety, depression, panic disorder, phobias and pain. This stew coloured my relationship with her and impeded the development of a warm mother-daughter bond. I sensed also that she was jealous of the closeness that existed between me and my father. I found her to be cold, judgemental, even cruel at times. She was on lots of medication. At home, she was a complex mother, wound-up tight with neuroses, caring but cold.

I have judged her harshly throughout my life but I am starting to feel some sympathy for her as I now have a better understanding of mental illness. If I had known about it when I was growing up, if there had been some sort of discussion, I might not have reacted so negatively to her. As it was, I resented the way she let her illnesses, both physical and mental, define her.

As she grew older, I resented the way she seemed to drain the life force out of my father. I couldn't accept that for her it was easier to become a sick person and be looked after than be a functioning woman who has to cope with life. She seemed to give up and that caused me to lose all respect for her. But I realise now that I am older and have had brushes with mental illness myself, that Mum was weighed down with accumulated grief but had no tools to deal with it. And that my father went along with her demands on him because he loved her. Perhaps I can even begin to forgive her.

I would love to know what she was like before life became too complicated for her.

To Your Only Daughter…Mum

You said 'you can't talk to boys
Boys are dirty'
You said 'don't wear black
Black is for tarts'

You said 'you'd look so much NICER
If you cut your hair
Long hair is messy'

You said 'be home early
Or I'll have a palpitation'

You were always in my face
But whenever I tried to get close
Saying 'let me do your hair, Mum'
You'd say 'don't touch my hair'
So I gave up
And walked away

And then one day
I'd just come home from school
First year high
I found you standing
In my room, Mum

You held up my diary
Unlocked and opened
You dragged me
Out the back
And down the yard
To the 44-gallon drum

> You poured on the petrol
> And said 'BURN IT.'
> And I did
>
> And I watched the innocent ramblings
> The first love secrets
> Flicker and burn
> Along with my respect
> For you, Mum

There were many other times when I felt her chill. It was the late 60s. I was just about to begin an arts degree when I fell pregnant. I was in a stable relationship with my boyfriend but not married and still living at home. We decided to be open and break the news to my parents, hoping for some support.

Instead my mother shrieked, 'How could you do this to me? What will people think? How can I face everyone?' and, clutching her ample bosom, proceeded to hyperventilate. Well, she must have worked out how to tell everyone because, on that very day, even though I was only just pregnant, she contacted all her family – my nana, and all the aunties and uncles – to share the disgrace. The news spread like wildfire. Needless to say, my poor boyfriend and I received no support. I was suitably shamed, shown to be the slut she had always feared. I was terrified.

My mother's solution to this scandal was to immediately announce our engagement, thereby ensuring my respectability (and hers).

Shortly after and possibly as a result of the tension and drama, my short-lived pregnancy ended up in the toilet as I went to pee. I had a miscarriage. If my mother had showed some restraint and waited, no one else would have been burdened with this dreadful news.

But the indignity didn't stop there. She decided that the right course of action was to immediately call the family doctor, who happened to be a strict Catholic. Instead of admitting me to hospital, or even to his surgery, he set about performing a curette right then and there in my childhood bedroom with no anaesthetic, to get rid of any remaining bits from my shameful pregnancy. I still remember the pain to this day.

But it wasn't just the physical pain. I can still hear my mother wailing outside my bedroom door as he was scraping my insides clean, 'See, this is your punishment.' There are some things that cannot be forgiven. Some words can never be unheard. My attitude to motherhood was forged that day.

I understand now the pressures she was faced with. She had given birth, seven years before me, to a little boy who grew up to be diagnosed as intellectually and developmentally disabled, 'mentally retarded' as it was called in those days. My brother had few social skills and consequently no friends. He was withdrawn as a child both with strangers and with his immediate family. I grew up with a ghost for a brother. In late adolescence, he developed schizophrenia.

My mother was unravelling. She became increasingly dependent on my father and on antidepressant medication.

But this was the 50s and nothing was ever discussed. I didn't understand what was happening around me, I just felt the effects.

It All Happened In Finlayson Street

> I grew up in the 50s in
> Finlayson Street, Netherby
> Where every night
> I'd put the billy out
> For the milkie
> And every morning
> I'd skim the cream
> Golden and gorgeous
> From the saucepan on the wood stove

I grew up in
The House That Dad Built
Post-war, with little money
But rich in skills
Dad made the bricks
And Mum, with me still inside her
Knelt on all fours
Nailing floorboards

I grew up in a house
Where politics was never discussed
I had to figure it out
For myself
And I did
While mum said
'Too good for us, are ya?
You're a radical
A bra burner
You're too independent'

I grew up in a house
Where sex was a dirty word
Brother's wet pyjamas
Nasty
Don't touch
Dirty
All a mystery to me

Where sex education
Meant getting marched
Down the backyard
To the pumpkin patch
'It's all about seeds and bees
Pollen and flowers,' Mum said
I found out another way

I grew up in a house
Where discussion was rare
Where narrow minds and prejudice
Were the order of the day
And comments like
'Don't suck that penny
A black man mighta touched it.'
Were common
And shameless

I moved on from that house
In Finlayson Street, Netherby
But there are shadows
From under its roof
That live in me
Still

Discussion was replaced with judgement. Conversation was reduced to 'What's for tea, which is cheaper Target or K-Mart, what was the food like at that motel, my lamingtons were better than hers, weren't they?' These were the dinner table discussions; it's no wonder I have always craved intellectual stimulation, which has led me down some rocky paths at times.

Meanwhile, the shadows were always lurking in the background.

I can relate so well to Gregory Crewdson's amazing photographs and David Lynch's films too. They tell of another world underneath what is shown to the everyday world. I realise that this exists in all families but I know that I have always been acutely aware of this real/pretend duality in my life growing up.

I wish that I had understood how mental illness had obviously shaped my mother's responses, physical and emotional, to her world; to her husband, her daughter, her son and to her friends and family.

Did she know that I resented her, did she even care if I did? With understanding comes forgiveness. Too late for her, but not for me.

4
Nana

My less than easy relationship with my mother was thankfully compensated in part by my Nana, who I find hard to believe was my mum's mother. Nana was one of the strongest, most positive influences in my early life. Unlike her daughter, she did not put much emphasis on a preoccupation with social correctness and pretence.

Born in the late 1800s, Nana grew up in a well-to-do German immigrant family in the south-east of South Australia. One of five children, four of whom were girls, she enjoyed family picnics in the countryside. All would be dressed in their Sunday best, the men in hats, formal suits and button-up shirts, the women in dark, heavy skirts, long-sleeved white blouses and the ubiquitous hat. I find it interesting that girls were permitted to ride bicycles back then, although I don't know how they did, wearing the long full skirts that were de rigueur, and on unsurfaced country roads. With fancy buggies drawn by a man riding a pushbike for the couples, horse-drawn carts for the families, these country picnics must have been both an opportunity to relax but also an opportunity to parade one's status.

Nana's father came as a baby with his family, along with many other German migrants in the mid-1800s, to the south-east from Adelaide, where he was born. He was well-respected in the community for his prowess in rifle shooting. Known as one of the best pigeon shots in the Commonwealth, for some time he even held the championship of Australia. He certainly looks the part in photographs taken at the time: an imposing figure in stylish waistcoat with sculpted beard and moustache, with his precious rifle always at hand, a dead pigeon at his feet. I am slightly comforted by the fact that the barbaric practice of using live birds as targets was outlawed because of public outcry in 1959.

At the age of nineteen, Nana married an English shopkeeper and gave birth to six children – three sons and three daughters. She also worked in her husband's general store, which was well-known in the area. I think this experience in the world of work is partly responsible for her becoming the wise, forward-looking, strong woman that I came to know and respect.

Tragically, one of the girls, my namesake, Barbara, died at the age of thirteen from a mystery illness known at the time as creeping paralysis. This story always haunted me as I was growing up. I was convinced I wouldn't make it past my teens. Lively and attractive, Barbara suddenly lost the ability to use her feet then her legs, then the rest of her body, until eventually she became immobilised and death followed. The progression was quite rapid.

There is an eerie similarity here. I recently discovered, to my horror, that creeping paralysis was the old-fashioned name for what is now known as MS, multiple sclerosis. I, the Barbara named after that poor girl, was diagnosed with MS just after turning fifty. Is this history repeating or is there some darker force at work? When I was first diagnosed, I was terrified that I would lose my mobility, or worse, but at least I was able to access information about my condition and discuss treatment options. How terrifying must it have been for my young aunt Barbara at a time when there was no explanation for her condition whatsoever. How I wish I knew more about her. MS remains a scary condition, as there is still no cure and no proven cause. It is unpredictable and totally random. I count myself lucky because my MS has not progressed. All my energies go into making sure it stays that way. I love my name but I forbid it to be passed down to any future granddaughters; it is easy to think of it as cursed. I reflect too that her untimely death must have had a traumatic impact on Nana and her other children, including my mother.

I have another odd connection to my ill-fated Aunt Barbara. Before she died, Nana gave me a large, elegantly framed photograph of Barbara as a little girl, her blonde hair in perfect ringlets. She also gave me a rather grim one the same size of her father, my great-grandfather, posing with his rifle and a dead pigeon. I proudly had both photographs hanging on the walls of my first home, a hundred-year-old cottage in the Adelaide Hills after I was married. The cottage burnt to the ground during the Ash Wednesday bushfires. My great-grandfather was spared but not Aunt Barbara: she was incinerated. Barbara's curse?

I felt closer to Nana than my mother in many ways. Unlike Mum, she didn't judge and I cannot remember a time when she said a harsh word to me. Even when I found myself young, pregnant and unmarried in the 60s, her response was extraordinary. Unlike my mother, who was spectacularly unsupportive in the whole matter, Nana encouraged me to go on the very recently developed contraceptive pill, which I found exceptional for someone her age. Having had no luck obtaining a prescription from my Catholic family doctor, I bought a cheap ring, pretended to be engaged and went to another doctor. On hearing about this, Nana told me not to worry about how to pay for it, that she would give me the money each month, which she did without ever letting on to my mother. It was our beautiful secret and I loved and respected her for it. She taught me the value of trust and unconditional love.

Her pragmatic approach to life was ahead of its time, but understandable given that she had worked hard, both in and out of home, raised five babies and buried one, all with little emotional support from her husband. I remember her words, 'I would get pregnant whenever your grandfather took his trousers off and laid them over the bedpost.' I remember him as cold, distant and unsmiling. I do not recall him speaking one word to me. He used to make money from horse racing, I believe he was a money-lender. I have always despised betting in any form, to me it symbolises the abuse of power and a preoccupation with material wealth. Horse racing in particular I find intolerable because of my stance on animal rights. I have never attended a horse race or bet money on anything, even a lottery ticket.

I can see that as a mother I have modelled myself on Nana, not my mother. Nana showed me acceptance, support and unconditional love.

She's the one I talked with, cooked with. I even slept in her room as her companion as she got older. She would accompany me on her piano while I sang old songs: 'Have you seen but a white lily grow?' and 'The Lost Chord'. She told me she used to accompany my grandfather, who apparently was quite the vocalist in his younger days. Strangely, I have no memory of Nana ever playing for my mother even though she sang so beautifully. I wonder about this. I also question why, if my grandfather used to enjoy singing, he didn't encourage my mother's singing aspirations. I find it hard to warm to the memory of my grandfather.

As a school student, I would often spend the night at Nana's place, where she would encourage my studies and exam preparation, saying, 'Don't stay up late studying, go to bed, set your alarm, get up really early in the morning and study when your brain is fresh.' That became my practice for many years, through university and into my teaching career.

I think my Nana would have fitted in nicely if she had been born into today's world.

5
Down The Cape

It was popular in the 1960s to buy or build a shack, a modest holiday home where the family could get away from the demands (and boredom) of the suburbs to commune with nature, albeit in often austere conditions.

A huge chunk of my childhood was spent in innocent bliss at our family shack – built by Dad of course, on the southernmost tip of the Fleurieu peninsula – that we called The Cape. Basic, really a glorified tin shed, it was magnificent in our eyes, boasting an uninterrupted view of the mysterious Kangaroo Island and beyond. Standing on top of the windswept cliff on which the shack was perched, I liked to think that there was nothing between me and Antarctica. The view was often extremely windy, sometimes cold and wet, sometimes scorching hot, but always beautiful. With no running water, bath, shower, oven or inside toilet, it was there I learnt what is important in life and what is not. There began my enduring love of nature and my deep affection and respect for animals, particularly sheep and cows.

If we were lucky, there would be dolphins in Backstairs Passage, engaged in their synchronised water ballet. Local fishermen would tell of sharks lurking menacingly near the shore. My eyes would follow the path of tankers as they slowly edged their way across the horizon. Small fishing boats scuttled out from the bay past the jetty in the mornings hoping for a good catch and returned as it grew dark. You knew when they had been successful, as seagulls swarmed noisily overhead, eager for scraps. No TV, no phone, no radio, just Freedom, Peace and Joy.

Freedom because as a young girl of nine or ten, I was allowed to walk unaccompanied far from the shack, leaping across the multicoloured jagged rocks that framed the shoreline, often singing to myself at full voice. There were no rules to prevent me from climbing cliffs, some made of fine white sand, some rocky, but all steep and dangerous. I would clamber to the top and gaze out to the horizon, scanning for pirate ships. I could run, sing and dream. It was where I learnt to be alone and treasure it.

The Cape brought Peace because I wasn't worried about anything while there. I realise now that it brought a welcome respite for me, an anxious child who used to regularly think about death and be brought low with the pain of migraines. Respite too for my parents, and my brother, from the demands and uncertainties of a tense life back in suburbia. All you could hear was the endless pounding of waves against the rocks, seagulls screeching, cows and sheep calling.

I experienced real Joy. I didn't need to seek out entertainment. The open paddocks, the animal bones, the driftwood, the lambs and poddy calves were all mine to enjoy. Why would I need more? Everything had a familiar warmth and a newness at the same time. Would there be tiny, translucent shrimps in the rock pool when the tide went out? Would a nonplussed cow come and stand watching me as I sat on the long drop toilet? Would I be able to make it around the rocks before the tide came gushing in, blocking my path? How many dolphins would I see passing by? Would I be blown off the cliff one day by the ever-present vicious wind? Would I see rabbits in the car headlights? Could I help churn the butter, milk the cows? Such richness.

A treat above all else would be when my dad took me with him jetty-fishing. I learned to cast the rod, bait the hook with gents – Dad's name for maggots – make the burley and sprinkle it onto the surface of the water to tempt the fish. I can still remember the pleasant, earthy smell. Even though I was constantly terrified of the ocean, dark blue beneath the wooden slabs of the jetty, I would reel in the poor fish: tommy ruff, the long, thin snook and my favourite, the leatherjacket. I learnt to deal with the black, oozy ink and sharp alien-like beak of the squid, the sharp spike on the leatherjacket, the skin, the scales and the guts. And there were plenty of fish to be caught then, before the coming of the greedy trawlers and nets. Dad and I would take the catch proudly back to Mum, who would fillet and cook them immediately: delicious!

Dad hated the frequent strong winds and on many a stormy night would take refuge in our car parked beside the shack. Maybe he didn't trust his building skills, but he shouldn't have worried, as the shack was bunker-like and would have stood firm in a cyclone. Maybe it was some other fear?

I think part of my soul is still there. The coastline is identical to the rugged coast of Cornwall from where my ancestors came. I wonder if that's what attracted my dad to this place, as this was his heritage. His grandfather had been captain of the Burra mines. I wish I could tell my parents how much I loved going there. I think it's no coincidence that I ended up in an apartment high on a hill overlooking a river, not a thunderous ocean but ever-changing water nonetheless. Again, I have an uninterrupted view of the sky and clouds with their many moods and colours. I think I would die without a view.

My brother exercised his freedom too. He would go for long walks along the coastline, loping along with his distinctive gait, eyes fixed ahead. He would set out in the morning and return in the late afternoon invariably sun or wind burnt or both. Mum kept an old metal ship's bell in the kitchen that she would ring to let him know when it was time to come home. He always seemed better down the Cape, not so agitated or frustrated. He lived to walk, then and for his entire adult life. I yearn to know what he was thinking about on those walks.

6
Brother

One of the saddest memories I have from my childhood is when I was quite small, maybe five or six, in infant school as it was called then. I was playing on the big spinner in the schoolyard with my friends when they asked me, 'Do you have any brothers and sisters?'

I will never forget my answer: 'No.' I didn't even stop to think about it; the No just came blurting out.

The incident must have pricked my conscience, because I reported it to my mother that evening.

Her response was devastating. 'How could you? Of course you have a brother.'

I still wear the shame to this day.

My brother, B, came into the world under a haze of stress, panic and probably guilt. Instead of being encouraged to push after experiencing the contractions of labour, my mother was ordered by nurses at the hospital to hold the pains in, to wait until the doctor arrived. He didn't arrive for some time, which led to my unborn baby brother, and undoubtedly my mother, experiencing a great degree of dangerous stress. Even worse, being deprived of vital oxygen at birth was thought to have contributed to my brother experiencing delayed intellectual development throughout his life.

If the trauma of his birth was not enough of a bad start, my brother spent the crucial first seven years of his life in an environment of relative sensory deprivation. Like many young couples during World War II, my parents could not afford to live independently, so lived with my mother's parents for a time. The shy, withdrawn little boy was not given free rein to play; rather he was frequently reprimanded by my authoritarian grandfather for making any noise. My brother never recovered from his bad start. Whether he had the tools to do so is a question that will forever go unanswered. However, what is clear is that the cards were stacked against him from the minute he attempted to draw his first breath.

Placed in a mainstream primary school, he was teased by his peers and humiliated by teachers. One teacher in particular regularly refused to allow the little boy to go to the toilet during lesson time. As a result, B would 'hold on' sometimes all day rather than face ridicule. He ended up having to have surgery as a child for a hiatus hernia.

He was no angel, though, becoming famous for the large number of metal ink nibs which he successfully would flick upwards so that they became impaled in the ceiling above him as he sat at his desk. Such acts of mischief would always be accompanied by a wide grin, infuriating his teacher.

Nevertheless, he learnt to read and write. In fact, he loved reading and had an amazing memory for random historical dates and many other seemingly inconsequential details, Rain Man-like. B, however, had very poor social communication skills. I often wonder if he had grown up today whether he would have been placed somewhere on the autism spectrum. He had no friends, was withdrawn and talked rarely. He seemed to live inside himself. Were those early signs of his schizophrenia developing?

I grieve for the big brother I never had: the companion, the playmate, the supporter, the role model. I grieve for the brother I did have: the looming shadow always present in my childhood and in my dreams.

I realise now how much he had taken from my parents too, unwittingly of course. Dad's lost dreams of a son, replaced by crushing responsibility, constant worry, vigilance and compromise. Mum's lost dreams of a son, replaced with shame, embarrassment, fear, frustration and anxiety. Possibly guilt too.

I grieve for his troubled life, his lack of connection. Did he get lonely or was his brain constantly full with things I have no knowledge of? I have no memory whatsoever of chatting or playing with him when we were growing up. He was always in his room by himself or down the backyard in the shed.

I grieve for his paranoia, his voices. He used to think that people on the radio were talking to him or about him. He would have imaginary conversations, talking softly to himself, often repeating over and over things that he had said or heard people say to him – 'Yes, Barb. Yes, Barb' – and ask the same questions: 'Is this book fact or fiction?'

I grieve for his disordered thoughts and frustrations which would regularly result in uncontrollable giggles or manic yelling, both of which have left me with emotional scars. He would giggle all the time, at meals, sitting on his own, in the car beside me on the back seat.

I am reminded of the decline of Syd Barrett, the tortured genius behind Pink Floyd who was brought down by schizophrenia. Syd is captured so brilliantly in the lines from 'Shine on You Crazy Diamond'. B too was a 'target for faraway laughter' and he would also get that look in his eyes 'like black holes in the sky'.

I wonder now why he was giggling. Could he hear something funny that I couldn't? Was he responding to the world around him in a way that was totally appropriate to his inner dialogue? I remember feeling left out, separated from his inner world. My brother was a stranger to me.

I giggle too when I am angry and frustrated, which still makes me extremely anxious. I panic that I am behaving like B and so I must have inherited his lack of self-control. I recall giggling, from nervousness no doubt, when Dad used to try to help me with my maths homework at the kitchen table. I hated doing that in front of my beloved dad. I think I was trying to be the perfect child.

The memory of the yelling goes to a deeper place; for me it symbolises witnessing scenes of conflict, usually between my brother and my mother. I will never forget those yells – they were the stuff of nightmares, ear-splitting wordless screams from a disturbed brain that would terrify me. B would yell so forcefully and for so long that for hours afterwards he would lose his voice. Sometimes he would vomit. I cannot help but reflect that B, a non-smoker, died of oesophageal cancer. Could this have been precipitated by the damage he had done to his throat over many years?

I know that this experience of growing up with my complex brother has contributed to my terror of personal conflict. Added to this is the fact that I was never given any explanations. After all, it was the 1950s, when complex things such as mental illness were never discussed with children. For that matter, they were hardly even discussed amongst adults. Consequently, I felt like I had no brother, that I lived with a ghost like Boo Radley. I learnt to be constantly on guard, ever-watchful, anticipating those random events. I found it difficult to relax and still do. Even now, I dislike cleaning my teeth because you can't hear what is going on around you. As a child, I remember being frightened that my brother would come into the bathroom without me realising he was there – he tended to move silently around the house in his padding, loping fashion. He was never violent towards me but I grew up in a state of puzzling hyper-vigilance, with my brother a mostly benign but unsettling presence and my mother always tense, often neurotic.

Saturday mornings were the worst. Dad worked as a barman at the races for extra money. That meant B was home with just me and Mum without the reassuring presence of my dad. Dad knew how to manage B. When he wasn't there, B grew bolder or perhaps more frightened. He would bait my mother and behave in ways that he knew would get a rise out of her. Typically, Mum would call out to him to summon him to the kitchen to have his lunch. There were times when he would stubbornly and coldly refuse, which would infuriate her. It would gradually escalate into an ugly standoff, which was scary to witness since my brother was a fully grown young man, not a little boy. Sometimes there would be the awful yelling. Often, he would reduce my mother to tears.

There began my tendency to catastrophise, I was always vaguely unsettled, worried that something bad was going to happen. One day something did: my brother attacked my father. With a hammer.

I would have been around eight years old. I heard about it from my parents. Indeed, it was one of the only times I was ever told what was going on. I was horrified and scared. Scared for my dad; scared for, and of, my brother; and scared for me. I think that this baseline fear and anxiety never left me. That was when I started getting migraines, or sick headaches as my mother used to call them. It was also when my brother had his first breakdown. After seeing a psychiatrist at Glenside Hospital, he was diagnosed with paranoid schizophrenia, with the complication of moderate intellectual impairment. He spent many years after this diagnosis going in and out of Glenside like through a revolving door. But again, I had to put the pieces together for myself: I saw all the medication. I was never included in any discussions on the matter; in those days, children were to be spared the realities of life, even when they were impacted. I could never ask my friends to sleep over or come to my house to play.

The collateral damage of living with this daily tension impacted on my whole family. I know I lived in a state of nervous anticipation, hyper-vigilance they call it. I was anxious, never knowing when there would be a blow-up, a scene, a conflict of wills.

I will always wonder if he was happy, what he thought about, what he felt? What did he think of me? *Did* he think of me? Why did he raise a hammer to my father, whom he adored?

I grieve for the drab, musty, vaguely menacing men's hostels he spent time in as he got older, that always stank of tobacco smoke. It was during the 1980s movement away from institutional to often inadequate community care – the awful 'rest homes' with impossible names like Daisy Nook. I recall him not receiving enough food at one such place and being told angrily that he had broken into their kitchen and eaten a whole cooked chicken. His endless collecting of random, worthless objects. Was he trying to fill an empty life or trying to make sense of the chaos inside his head? As Patrick Pound said, 'To collect is to gather your thoughts through things.'

We were all bruised by the locked ward at Glenside, the tablets, the hormone injections, the shock treatment, the endless appointments with psychiatrists, the run-ins with police, the unseen things.

I grieve for his death, horrible yet mercifully quick.

We fear what we don't understand; perhaps if I had been given more information, more relevant conversation as I was growing up, I would not have been so anxious about the world around me. I realise now I must have soaked up the surrounding constant tension, worry and fear when I was a child.

As it was, that general feeling of unease and confusion prompted in me a desire to escape and explore a bigger world than the one I was brought up in.

7
Escape – Music and Uni

Music has been a big part of my life since I was a little girl obsessed with the music of Prokofiev and Tchaikovsky. I learnt to appreciate many forms of music during the seven years I took ballet and piano classes. I also enjoyed participating in singing competitions. Maybe I inherited some of my mother's singing ability.

But the Beatles definitely were the major music experience in my early teens. Like many other young teenage girls at the time, I was in a little gang of girls and had my favourite Beatle; mine was John. I had the vinyl, the sketchbooks filled with fan pictures, I even had the haircut. I would pretend to be John and mimic the way he stood and played his guitar, peering short-sightedly into the distance. Their sound was magic; it spoke to my baby boomer generation, where everything was new, where the old was being thrown out. Our parents had battled during the war and the Depression and had lived with austerity, deprivation and tradition. The Beatles seemed to slide into this new slot: fresh, joyful and fun with just enough disregard for convention but not too much. The real rebellion came later; we were still too young to press the envelope too far.

The harder, darker side started to filter through to me as I got older. In my late teens and through university years, Bob Dylan became huge in my life and his impact has continued to this day. It was as though he woke us up to what was going on in the world: racial prejudice, war, injustice. He seemed to challenge the status quo. Dylan's music didn't just bring just a new feeling and sound, it held thoughts, concepts, philosophies, poetry, it had depth and so much meaning. I was drawn to his poetry as I was to the French poets, writers and philosophers, from Baudelaire to Proust. Dylan was like a drug; I was transported by his music. He seemed to speak to our disaffected generation who had begun to question what their world was offering and had found that it couldn't give them the answers they needed. He had the genius and the balls to express these questions in his songs.

My love affair with rock music gradually became darker and heavier till I was immersed in Black Sabbath, Deep Purple, Pink Floyd and Led Zeppelin.

I still like to mix it up in black leather at a Metallica, Malmsteen or Rammstein concert, surrounded by scary-looking metal heads or dreadlocked musos. I feel equally at home in the formal elegance of the Opera House swooning to the Sydney Symphony Orchestra or grooving to the neo-psychedelics of Tame Impala. Always open to the music, I believe stagnation is ageing. Like another personal hero David Bowie, I attempt to reinvent myself as each stage of my life morphs into the next. Music comes along for the ride. Or does it provide the vehicle?

I was fortunate to score entry into Yoko Ono's appearance at the opening of her exhibition *War is Over*, at the MCA. It was as though my past and my present were converging.

White Fedora

> The hot pink room is intense
> We all radiate warmth and anticipation
> We breathe in communal joy
> We are going to be in this space
> With Yoko Ono
> The Woman from John Lennon's song
> Is this what out-of-body feels like?
>
> She's here
> Tiny. Fragile yet strong
> Iconic. Yet very real
> A white fedora frames her ageless beauty
> We crane our necks to catch a glimpse
> A force from our collective history
> Is standing right here

Speaking to us
Of love and wishes
Possibilities and peace
She moves us all
From Michael Kirby, himself a hero
To actors and artists
The old and the young

To those like me who remember
Marching through the streets singing
Give Peace a Chance
I feel a frisson from those heady days
Filled with hopes and dreams
War Is Over If You Want It
We need this message today

Take home a piece of sky
From a soldier's helmet
Tie a wish to a tree
Write a message to your mother
Mend something that is broken
Play chess with only white pieces
Choose peace not war

We walk down the hot pink carpet
Into the tropical night
Lightning sheets across the Harbour
Thunder rumbles at Circular Quay
Fireworks illuminate the Opera House
This night has been touched by magic
Or perhaps the power of our wishes

University presented me with many opportunities to escape and explore.

Those days were heady. Times were achanging, the atmosphere was electric in a beautiful way, it was all rainbows not thunderstorms. The hippie culture, flower power, the back-to-nature movement, psychedelic music, all focused on experiencing new things, new ways of thinking, seeing and feeling. We wanted to change the world and we thought we could. We were young, naïve and blissfully innocent and the hippie lifestyle was extremely appealing. Experimenting with mind-altering drugs went hand in hand with this life force: we thought we could experience a new reality, a new consciousness by taking them. I think that's the difference between then and now. We took drugs because it was part of the hippie package not because we wanted to escape our lives; on the contrary, we were in love with life, we just wanted to experience it more deeply.

My experiences were mainly with marijuana, rolling and smoking joints, passing them round with friends, and smoking hash in a long carved wooden pipe. We experimented with magic mushrooms that we gathered from the wild. Nothing else, thank God. We had friends who had been admitted to psychiatric hospitals after taking LSD and, having had experience of such places through my brother, I found that concept terrifying so steered clear of it. Of course, there was alcohol too, but I have never had much success with that and it certainly didn't lead to fun or enlightenment; for me, it always led to a headache.

Pot, as we called it in those days, for me was rarely anywhere near mind-expanding, or even all that pleasurable. In fact, more often than not, I would become quite paranoid. I think drugs just highlight what is already there in your mind and your personality and, because I was always baseline anxious, that side of me became amplified. I recall a few experiences where visuals became brighter, more enhanced, and there were times when I thought I had discovered a new level of understanding about the world, but they were few and far between. I did it because it was cool.

I remember being visited by the drug squad while stoned and having to hide the stash, try to appear calm and normal until they left. I was freaking out. We grew our own marijuana plant along a creek so we wouldn't have to water it and thereby risk being seen. It grew so well it became enormous, so we eventually cut it down, stuffed it into the back of our VW Beetle (it took up the whole car) and drove it back to our cottage in the Hills. However, we never got to consume the monster because I was terrified of being raided by the cops. We would have had enough pot to be classed as dealers so I made the decision to get rid of it. We burnt the entire plant that night in our fireplace.

Magic mushrooms were another matter entirely. Easy to get, you only needed to know what to look for and where they grew, and, being free, they became a favourite. Cooked in pies, raw on crackers, they tasted pretty disgusting but you sort of got used to the taste and look of the tiny, slimy, bluish fungi. They were definitely mind-altering: hallucinogenic, scary and very dangerous. I remember one particularly bad trip where I thought my head was detaching from my body, literally. I have never been so terrified, and it seemed to last forever. I also recall being fascinated by the bright light from electric light bulbs, and I would stare at them for hours. Afterwards, every time I tried to read, all I could see was a really bright white after-image like you see when you accidentally look at the sun. As it wasn't going away and I was trying to study at the time, I told my mum and she bundled me off to an eye specialist who of course said, 'Have you taken any drugs?' My innocent negative reply didn't fool him and he promptly treated me for toxic poisoning. I was lucky I didn't lose my eyesight. Psilocybin is not to be taken lightly.

Interestingly, there was a type of alcohol that I found to have a similar effect as pot or hash. That was ouzo, the Greek aniseed-flavoured spirit. I have recently discovered why. It is very strong alcohol and, to avoid becoming seriously intoxicated, traditionally should be drunk over a period of time with mezes, small meals. No wonder I felt so stoned, as I probably had had nothing to eat at all. Perhaps it was the absinthe effect?

I also confess to, rather pompously, indulging in smoking French cigarettes, Gauloises and Gitanes, unfiltered of course. I still recall how they smelt, intensely perfumed like incense, but not as sweet. The thick ropey smoke would curl up through my fingers and past my lips, very French bohemian and ostentatious. I also became adept at rolling my own cigarettes using Tally Ho papers and Drum tobacco, again all purely for effect. I cringe now that I was so easily led. Was I trying to fit in, find an identity, or just aiming to please?

I genuinely loved the intellectual stimulation that was everywhere at uni. It was as though I was at last learning how to think, to discuss, reason, form an argument. I also thrived on the rigour, the structure and the discipline of academic study. The work didn't come easily to me; I had to work and work to keep up to the standard of my peers, most of whom seemed far more intelligent than me; in fact, some were brilliant. I was certainly not brilliant but I was determined, organised and a hard worker and those things got me through.

As I majored in English and French, I was able to study the same texts in English and in their original French, which I found most rewarding like *The Outsider* (*L'Etranger*) and *Waiting for Godot* (*En Attendant Godot*). It was a thrill to see how a translated text was originally written.

I loved the rigour of text analysis with its almost obsessive attention to detail, so it's no wonder I became a French and English teacher. I was terrified however, of my French tutor, Madame G. I was silently self-conscious about my proficiency in spoken French so would desperately try to make myself as small and inconspicuous as possible in tutorials, so as to avoid being asked to answer a question or give my opinion, in French of course. This discomfort with fluency in spoken French, although not with the grammar or pronunciation, has stayed with me. I still try to avoid speaking to French speakers, fearing being discovered as a fraud.

I adored my French poetry lecturer, an immensely good-looking young man who would produce the most sensuous readings of Baudelaire and Verlaine.

I love research; I have an unquenchable thirst to find out new information, maybe because of the lack of discussion in my younger years. These were times well before the Internet, so research had to be carried out by digging through large books, periodicals and essays, retrieved from the dark, musky depths of the library basement. Strangely, I quite enjoyed this cloistered environment and often chose to write my essays down there, as the hallowed, safe privacy allowed my brain to focus fully on the task at hand.

I had realised in my early teens that I did not believe in a God of organised religion and wanted to place this lack of belief into a framework of understanding. I discovered philosophy and studied the subject with relish for two years. I struggled with Kant and Mill, Plato and Aristotle, but above all with existentialism and the existence of God. I fell in passionate, unrequited love with my philosophy lecturer; how could someone be so attractive both mentally and physically? I think it became an unreachable quest for the rest of my life.

These were exciting times too, of social unrest where everything was being challenged. Change was in the air. Australian forces were still in Vietnam and, much as the war was abhorred by most of us students, the other issue was that young guys were being called up. If your number was drawn in the lottery, that was it, you were in, unless you had valid reason not to go. Young men would get married, claim they were pacifist or go underground in order to dodge the draft. My boyfriend had his plan: if his name was drawn, he was going to starve himself in the hope of being deemed physically unfit for duty (he was already underweight).

The war came right into our living rooms every night on the TV news in ghastly reality, not the sanitised version the media allows us to see now. We saw the destruction of the Vietnamese people and their country, the stream of bombs and toxic chemicals like napalm being dropped on villages of women and children. We saw the brutality and it all seemed so senseless – what was the point? We didn't buy what we were being fed by our government and its boss, the USA. We, like many, many other students and other informed, caring people across the world, protested. Uni was definitely the place to be in those years. We would sit on the library lawns with our placards, listening to speeches, being inspired, we felt like we were part of a much larger world movement or consciousness. It was delicious; we knew what we were doing was right but we also knew it was going against the status quo and therefore dangerous and rebellious. We decided to stand up and not be silent.

Moratorium 1970 we took it to the streets. We felt like we were at least doing something; that silence was, and is, consent.

I had never experienced anything quite like the feeling of being in a large, organised group of people all with the same goal, the same idea, marching together in the streets of the city I grew up in. Traffic was stopped, onlookers were either cheering us or hurling abuse. We sang 'All we are saying is Give Peace a Chance' and I still cannot hear that John Lennon anthem without the memories flooding back with the sounds, the tears, the soaring feelings, the feeling of power. It was electric. I can understand the attraction of binding together with like-minded others to express your views, your anger and frustrations. It is a powerful driving force, almost primal. Social media satisfies that drive now, I think.

I wish that I had then the understanding of politics that I do now, but I had never studied any history, politics or economics. Nevertheless, I knew I was against war, as I still am today.

I must admit to feeling ashamed that I was disrespectful to the soldiers who fought in Vietnam. I did not have the emotional maturity and intellectual balance to grasp that they were just doing their job. It wasn't their war; it was the politicians, the multinational corporations, the power-brokers, the arms manufacturers who were driving it. I'm sorry for that. So many of those soldiers were, as some still are, deeply scarred by what they had seen, heard and done. And to add to their trauma, they were disrespected and rejected by young people like me.

8
Schooldays

I liked the mental stimulation of school but, most of all, I enjoyed the rigour, the organisation. Why did I enjoy this structure? Was it a contrast to the unpredictability of life at home?

This capacity was recognised early by my teachers. At primary school, I quickly became 'headmaster's pet', or rather slave/unpaid assistant. It wouldn't be allowed these days but back in the 50s things were pretty basic; I doubt whether teachers or even school principals had the luxury of assistants. I would like to think that was the only reason I was regularly summoned to his office on the school PA: 'BJ, come to my office straight away.' Nothing dubious ever occurred but I must have been seen by my fellow students as at best a goody-goody, at worst a monumental suck. I would spend whole lessons printing out his teaching and administration material, turning the handle on the trusty Gestetner machine, the 50s precursor of the photocopier. I still remember the smell of the ink on my fingers and the clunking sound the machine made as it spewed forth the pages. I received no payment or rewards of any kind for this time-wasting lack of instruction. Perhaps it was seen by teachers, and perhaps some students, as a badge of honour.

My school had some fiercely authoritarian teachers who maintained discipline and daily order by using sarcasm, bullying, shaming and the cane. They were hated and feared by all the students. Others were lovely, firm but fair like Mrs S, who inspired me to gain the honour of dux in grade 5. We would walk to her house before school, play marbles on the footpath until she came out, then walk with her to school. She allowed herself to be seen as a real person who truly liked and cared for her students. I'm sure I modelled myself on Mrs S when I became a teacher some years later.

It was at this school that I met a beautiful, shy, blonde-haired girl named A, newly arrived from Germany. I had never met anyone who spoke a foreign language. We connected instantly. She taught me to sing 'Silent Night' in German, which I still can; maybe it was the beginning of my lifelong love of languages.

But that was not all. I was in awe of her ability to draw; my first experience of someone with artistic ability and sensibility. She quickly became my best friend and we have been best friends ever since. She became an accomplished artist and I went on to become a language teacher. I have surrounded myself with art, artists and art teachers throughout my life. I find it fascinating to whom we are attracted: where does it come from? Our influences early in life are so important but I question whether I was influenced by the things I saw in A or whether I was drawn to her because I already had an innate interest in those talents that she possessed.

As a brainy teacher's pet, I was given the task of rehabilitating naughty boys. A poor runty lad with the unfortunate name of Wayne was forced to sit next to me in the hope that some of my goodness would possibly rub off. What did rub off was a blissfully rude song that he taught me which I still remember:

> I'm Popeye the Sailor Man
> I live in a caravan
> With a hole in the middle
> Where I do my piddle
> I'm Popeye the Sailor Man

Perhaps that was where my interest in naughty boys began.

Primary Days

> Sipping warm milk
> from tiny thick glass bottles
> cream underneath their silver caps
> Fritz and sauce sandwiches

Turning sliced white bread to red mush
Twirling a fluorescent musk lolly between my lips
as sharp as a hypodermic
Choo Choo bars that turned my mouth
from pink to black
Slurping a meat pie
from a brown paper lunch order bag
the juice dribbling down my chin
onto my grey serge uniform
Monitors for everything
flag, blackboard, tuck shop
Ink, lunch, homework
everyone got a turn
Daily assembly
singing the National Anthem
while the Aussie flag was raised
Marching single file
into the classroom
to the beat of the drum and fife band
Post-war regimented
Odd games with elastics and string
Skipping into a long rope
I could never get it right
couldn't get the rhythm
The terrifying jungle gym,
too high for me and rusting
Where the confident kids were king
the whizzy that always tried to hurl me off
The ancient long seated swing
pierced with splinters
No shade no grass no trees
just scratchy black asphalt
melting on hot days
scoring a bloody thatch on your knee
The shelter shed where we dutifully sat
on long narrow benches

munching our sandwiches
and drinking our milk
Pigtails dipped in inkwells
by the naughty boy sitting behind
naive courting behaviour
Heavy wooden desks
with curved iron legs
and tattooed with initials
that should have read

Uniformity
Conformity
Compliance

I can see so clearly that being the late 50s, only a few years had passed since the world had been rocked by World War II. Here was Freedom but it must have seemed tenuous. Society was happy but scared to disturb any sleeping giants.

My local high school, even though a public school, functioned in many ways like a private school. Status was all-important, so rules were strict, classes were graded and students were ranked according to ability. We were subjected to intelligence tests, weekly headmaster's tests, private-school-style uniforms, strong discipline, chalk and talk, segregation of the sexes and little tolerance of diversity, with university entrance the ultimate goal. I did not enjoy my high school years; I found them rigid and tinged with cruel sarcasm.

My primary school years of accepting and even relishing the structure that comes with uniformity had faded. Now I bucked the rules at every possible opportunity, especially when it involved uniforms. Girls were lined up and made to kneel as a teacher measured how far the skirt reached above the knee; there was a strict regulation length. We got around that by blousing our box-pleated tunics way up above the belt. My skirt was, as a result, alarmingly short. After all, miniskirts were the fashion at the time: think Twiggy. We were supposed to wear regulation neat white shirts but I chose to wear one of my dad's shirts, resulting in a suitably messy, unkempt look. After school, prefects would harass me as I walked home hatless and gloveless. Should I have cared?

The school had boys and girls but they were kept separate; my first experience of segregation. There was an imaginary line running through the school grounds which we were not allowed to cross. Heaven forbid that we might be caught talking to a boy.

We couldn't leave the school grounds without permission. I would flout that rule, sneaking out at lunchtime to saunter up to the local shop with my friends to escape the prison and meet boys. Of course, we were seen, reported and hauled up to the office of the headmistress.

I have a particularly vivid memory of one such lecture and I think I know why the scene has stayed so intact in my memory.

There we were, three young girls, standing silent in Miss P's office, trying to appear contrite in front of her desk while she berated us. Rather than feeling frightened or intimidated, I was bemused and detached. My eyes were fixed on the small vase of bright red camellias on her desk, when suddenly one of the flower heads detached from its stem and fell, PLOP, onto the carpet below. I couldn't help myself, I burst into loud giggles, ruining the solemnity of the occasion. Miss P grudgingly let us off with a frosty warning.

I have reflected on this scene many times and I think it says a lot about my attraction to the absurd, and my tendency to nervous laughter. I'm sure my reaction would have been different if I had real feelings of respect and affection for the school, its rules and Miss P.

There were, however, teachers at the school whom I loved, respected and consequently worked hard for. They were generous with their time and genuinely interested in me, not just in my marks. I learnt much from those teachers.

Most were simply there to toe the department line and to uphold and maintain academic traditions. Some were downright cruel, sarcastic and spiteful. I'm sure that my attitudes to teaching were conceived and shaped during my years as a student at this school. In one of the many ironies that would pepper my life, this school was the first to which I was appointed when I graduated. I cried real tears. I went from school to uni and then back to the same school again. I stayed for my bonded three years, after which I transferred out.

There were highlights, however. I met my first steady boyfriend, whom I went on to marry and have two children with. I also fell in love with the French language, English literature and writing. I went on to study French and English at uni, then taught them, and I still love to write.

9
From Aldgate Valley To St Kitts

Aldgate Valley. Those two words instantly flood me with warmth. As soon as I married at age twenty-one, I moved from living with my family in the suburbs to my hippy idyll, a small stone cottage on a hillside in the Adelaide Hills. I realise this was my second view – not the ocean this time but green paddocks pocked with wild blackberries, bracken and heath. Freed from the limits of the suburbs and in love, I thought it was heaven.

I realise now how lucky I was to be in that situation at that age. It is almost impossible these days for a young couple to buy their own home. The tide has almost turned back to what it was like for my parents after the war, when many were forced to live with their parents. Where will the pendulum swing next?

I had always loved animals and in Aldgate Valley that love was allowed to grow. It started with one black puppy named Spike and one black sheep, creatively named Blackie. This animal obsession quickly grew to big black dogs with Shakespearean names like Brutus and Tybalt, to sleek, aloof Weimaraners with German names, Jaeger and Elsa.

We kept chickens too, rearing bantams in the kitchen, watching with great excitement as the chicks bravely cracked open their shells. One of my sweetest pleasures was walking down the hill to the chook house to collect the eggs. It always seemed such a miracle. I learnt with relish about all the different types of hens and roosters.

There were other more unwelcome residents on our little farm: rats, foxes and snakes, even the deadly brown, but mostly the big fat, glossy red-bellied blacks. The rats came to eat the sheep nuts and the snakes came to feed on the rats. Foxes, although exquisitely beautiful, are merciless, cruel killers. If a lamb was born during the night, it had to be strong to survive the vicious attacks of a fox. Many a morning,

I would go out to the paddock to find a newly born lamb, perfect in every way except with its head ripped off and tongue eaten or tragically complete except for its heart. I used to think how distressing it must have been for the mother ewe who had just given birth. Wild dogs were a problem too, probably pets gone feral, their attacks vicious and gruesome, as they would attack in packs.

But by far the most memorable unwanted visitor was one thirsty black snake. I was sitting at my spinning wheel in the lounge room of our cottage, enjoying the sunshine. My fingers greasy with lanolin, I was enjoying the rhythm of combing the wool, pulling it out, feeding the fine strands into the wheel while my foot pressed gently up and down, up and down. Mesmerised by the rhythmic turning of the wheel, my eyes suddenly came back into focus as they detected something black and shiny sliding behind the bookshelf. Was it a millipede – they were in plague numbers? No, it was too big. I realised with horror it was a snake, a black snake in my lounge room. Scared now as my baby was asleep in his cot in another room, I searched through all the house for the intruder but found nothing. I prayed that the snake had made a getaway but, unconvinced, I called Wildlife Rescue.

Shortly after, a khaki jeep pulled into my driveway and out jumped a khaki man straight from a TV nature programme. He had all the necessary implements for rescue and recovery, he looked the part, he earnestly searched the house, but no snake. He convinced me that the serpent had left the building then bundled up his gear and left.

My husband came home from work, heard my story of the day's events and dutifully performed yet another house search to allay my anxieties. Meanwhile, I went to the toilet for a pee. Ahhhhhhh. My yell could have been heard in Tasmania. There was the snake, thick, black and shiny curled around inside the toilet bowl, looking up at me. I leapt up in horror and screamed for help. My husband grabbed the shovel that we kept beside the back door in case of snakes, charged into the little toilet room and proceeded to chop at the poor snake in a frenzy, complete with loud karate-style shouts. The lino floor was never the same again.

I was grateful that the danger had passed but I missed the khaki man, who would have carefully retrieved the poor, frightened creature, popped him/her into a khaki canvas bag to be later released into the wild to live another day. The unfortunate reptile was probably thirsty and had slid into the bowl looking for water as we were in the middle of a drought. I must have peed with the snake below. I could not pee in that toilet for a long time but I had gained a fabulous party story.

But, above all, there were the sheep. The sheep obsession began with Blackie, a stout brown Ryeland ewe, as tame, docile and affectionate as a pet Labrador. I could take her for walks on a lead; she would come when called and nuzzle into me with her beautiful woolly head. I become obsessed easily and so one sheep became two until we were the proud owners of the largest coloured sheep flock in South Australia. I researched all I could find on sheep management and history. Fascinated by all the breeds – Merino, Corriedale, Polwarth, Poll Dorset, Border Leicester, we had them all.

I soon discovered that sheep are not stupid as is commonly thought, that they are as individual as dogs, with their own personalities and temperaments and very easy to tame. They were all named – many Shakespearean like our dogs: Macduff, Duncan, Romeo and Juliet. I learnt about shearing, dipping, drenching, fly strike and pinkeye. I witnessed life's dramas: birth, death, disease, joy and pain. I learnt to love the sounds, sights and smells of the shearing shed, learning to throw and sort a fleece with the musky thickness of lanolin ever present in the air.

Even though we both had regular jobs in the city during the week, we were living a semi-hippy lifestyle. We embraced the back-to-nature ethos, so I learnt to spin, weave, dye, crochet and knit the wool that we collected from our beautiful sheep.

Naturally coloured wool from so-called black sheep was hard to get and highly prized in this alternative lifestyle market. 'Coloured' wool was difficult to source since the traditional wool market was not interested in it. In fact, farmers would dispose of any lambs or sheep that showed any trace of it. The slightest bit of black in a wool clip would lower the value of the whole clip. Coloured sheep not only had little value but were vehemently shunned or kept separate from the rest of the flock as pets. If they did manage to reach adulthood, they ended up in the abattoir yards, where they were sold off cheap. We took advantage of the practice and in so doing saved many lives. We would go to the sale yards and search the pens for black sheep. I would sit perched on the railings, the only female surrounded by burly butchers and farmers, and wait for the auctioneer to call out, 'Dollar off for the black.' We would then transport the fortunate creatures in luxury back to the green hills of Aldgate. Transport wasn't a cruel semi-trailer but a jaunty Volkswagen Beetle to begin with and later a bright red mail van. Suffice to say these vehicles needed a hose-out after each transfer.

The first sheep we acquired this way we named Lucky, for obvious reasons. He was a big, rangy steel-grey Merino wether. I don't know if they were grateful but all these rescued sheep were very easy to tame and train. We had no need of sheep dogs or motorbikes; these gentle, woolly animals would come when called and follow us anywhere as long as we rattled the container of sheep nuts. Indeed, Lucky quickly became the leader of the whole flock.

Word got around that we had coloured sheep and were selling the wool. Soon we became quite well-known. In fact, the *Sunday Mail* featured a double-page spread on our venture. Customers could choose what sort of wool they wanted – fine, coarse, long, short, straight or wavy – and the colour, from white to grey, brown to black. They were provided with the name and breed of the sheep that the wool came from.

We always ran at a loss but it was worth it. I grew to love my time at the spinning wheel; it was definitely one of the most relaxing pastimes I have ever engaged in. Rather like meditating, there is a hypnotic rhythm of foot on pedal, combined with the gentle teasing, pulling, drawing the strands of wool through your hand, over and over again. Add to this the intoxicating, musky perfume of the raw wool and the waxy, sensuous massage of lanolin on fingers and I was transported to hippy heaven.

Long-staple wool was in high demand by hand spinners as it is easier and quicker to spin, so we decided to try to breed black Border Leicesters as their wool would be long in the staple, locally produced and marketed, and coloured as a bonus. We hoped to create a niche market. When we began, I had never seen a black Border Leicester. The white ones look like Greek gods with their aquiline profiles and flowing white robes. We were lucky enough to find a black Border Leicester ram that the owners (stud breeders) agreed to part with, invested in some white Border ewes and we were away. Or should I say Laddie the ram was away.

At the beginning, the small acreage at Aldgate was sufficient but of course, as the obsession grew, so did the need for more land. We settled on a property of a hundred and fifty acres that was perfect for grazing sheep because of its drier climate. Perhaps it was my German heritage but I fell in love with the country as soon as I set eyes on it. The magnificent rolling hills, just on the outer fringe of the Barossa Valley, were so peaceful as they stretched out to the horizon and down to the creek with its massive river gums and screeching galahs. Huddled around an open fireplace in the old German settler's cottage, which came with the land, watching tiny swallows soar and swoop, we felt like pioneers. As we walked among the derelict pig sheds thatched with straw and listened to the mournful calls of crows, it wasn't difficult to imagine what life was like there in earlier days. We found old farm equipment and delicate doilies, hand-made for protecting jars of jams and preserves from flies.

There was so much work to be done, and we loved every minute of it. From lifting and carrying bales of hay, caring for the sheep, hammering in star droppers, rolling out the cyclone wire, pulling it taut, straining it, cutting it with pliers, the work was endless. But I was young and strong and in love with the life.

Unfortunately, nothing lasts forever and after successive droughts and the fact that I had become pregnant and couldn't do the heavy work any more, we reluctantly decided to sell. The golden times were over.

I used to say that if there was a revolution, an apocalypse, I would be able to survive, having learnt many of the skills necessary for a self-sufficient lifestyle. I never again felt so real.

Those times cause me to reflect on the preoccupation of our society with the binary. Black/White. Value/Diminished Worth. Mainstream Culture/Counter Culture. Diversity/Status Quo. Left/Right. Gay/Straight. Male/Female. Pleasure/Pain. Love/Hate. I have always veered to the ideological and political Left of this divide, with this thread following me throughout my life, shaping my views and actions, my career and passions, my friends and my lovers.

Determined not to be my mother, I have aimed for the opposite of judgement. Acceptance, tolerance, compromise at all costs. This path has led me to many wonderful interactions but also to some disastrous ones. Fearing conflict, I have sacrificed assertiveness for peace. In one such relationship, I lost myself.

10
Lost

All my gut instincts screamed NOOOOOOO. I found him unattractive, conservative, right-wing, too smooth.

Even my mother took a dislike to him, saying, 'His lips are thin, a sign of cruelty.'

If only I had heeded her warning. Sucked in by his charm, I didn't go with my gut. He was different, quirky, he made me laugh. He was full of stories and that side of him reminded me of my dad. I think I wanted him to be my dad.

He knew what buttons to press; he made me feel special, kept telling me I was gorgeous, giving me the impression he could solve any problem, fix anything. He was not fazed by the fact that I had children, he was a 'make it happen' kind of guy, full of health and vitality, a fitness freak. He had an independent mind, not swayed by the crowd; he had never smoked, drunk alcohol or taken drugs. He wasn't afraid to go against authority and follow his own path. He was an individual. He seemed destined for great things and I found that hugely attractive.

What I didn't see were the red flags. The grandstanding, the relentless persistence, the unusual, rather disturbing sense of humour, the love of teasing, the sense of superiority. The patterns of odd behaviour, his inappropriate, vaguely sexual, relationships with much older women. His attachment to, yet hatred of, gay men. His undeveloped concept of boundaries in many areas, but in particular those that involved sexuality.

He was extremely, overly generous in situations which, by being so, made him look good to others. He held grudges. He appeared tough but it was a mask; he was thin-skinned and would take offence in a flash. He got angry, a lot. He would never accept blame; when things went wrong, they were always someone else's fault. He was funny, but his humour was off-centre, often at someone else's expense, prejudicial, coarse, vulgar, dark.

I have always admired individuality and I mistook his ways for that. I fell for his charms, his originality, his apparent devotion to me. I had never known anyone like him before, so I fell hard. He seemed special, one of a kind, and I felt I was lucky to have him.

I don't know whether it was love or fear that caused my inertia, my blindness to these flags. All I know is I lost myself in this man. My shame is that it took me so long to find myself again, even though so much damage had been done.

Thank You

Thanks for the fear
Ever present till your death
The dread the guilt
That I allowed you
Into my life
To trample
Me
My family
My friends

Thanks for the shame I carry
For my weakness
For my blindness to the truth
For so long
For getting sucked in
To your destructive vortex
Over
And over
And over
Again

Like a Panzer tank
You created carnage in your wake
Everyone I hold most dear
Affected by your need
For power for control
Your incomprehension
Of boundaries
My son
Refusing to be sucked into your web
Saw through you from the start
Enduring constant battles
Which have left their mark

My daughter
Too young to understand
Struggled to grasp what was going on
Confused by what love meant
She chooses wisely now

But above all my baby daughter
Your only daughter
Your own flesh and blood
Tossed emotionally
Relentlessly
Like a cork on a rough sea

Longing for your love
But receiving only scraps
You would disappear
Then reappear like Santa
Larger than life
Full of promises
Never kept
You hurt her worst of all
She almost lost herself too

> Your time bomb finally detonated
> I knew it would
> Nothing as dramatic as an
> IED in a war zone
> Your preference for sure
> No, your life choices were
> Your undoing
>
> I struggle hard for
> Positive memories
> Exhausted, I let go, I let you go
> Now light can overcome darkness
> And a lotus flower emerges
> A new woman
> Unafraid and strong

It is hard to cope with death at the best of times, but at the worst of times, it becomes almost impossible.

How do you grieve someone you despised, someone who filled you with dread?

Funeral

> Approaching the familiar church
> I panic
> I feel sick
> I can't do this.
> Negative energy radiates
> From the cold white walls
> As all their eyes
> Suddenly turn towards me

My plan is to radiate my own energy
Create a shield that will protect me
No expression
No tears
No eye contact
My rigid body silently is screaming
Approach at your peril.

The funeral director
Sombre and safe in his black suit
Leads me down the aisle
I have walked so many times
In peaceful reflection
Now the air is heavy
With an unholy fog

Unspoken animosity curdled
With silent aggression
Flanked by friends
I feel momentarily safe
But the coffin is too close
The eulogy too long
The sickly sweet hypocrisies
Build and build

I squirm, my breath is shallow
I struggle to remain in my seat
Everything inside me tells me to
Shout   Yell   Protest
Lay bare the other side of this
Oh so shiny coin
The unpolished side
But I sit silent

My eyes are fixed on the coffin
Now wreathed with incense
I try to send out my last communication
Anger yes, but sadness too
How to reconcile?
The damage done
The possibilities forever lost

11
Dealing With Damage

Like everyone, I have had to learn to live with damage. I strive to go against the odds and the cards which I have been dealt. I have come to understand that damage comes in many forms and at unexpected times.

Undoubtedly, the most prolonged, insidious, destructive damage in my life has been from living with migraines.

I become anxious very easily. In fact, I think it can be my resting state if I am not constantly on the lookout for the signs. Unfortunately, my way of coping with stress has been to get a migraine, which effectively shuts me down so I don't have to interact any more. I saw my mother do it many, many times as I was growing up. It is of course an extremely self-destructive, if effective, behaviour.

I realise that migraines are probably a symptom of other damage, but they cause untold damage as well. The searing pain, the enforced isolation and the accompanying loneliness have haunted me like an ever-present shadow since I was nine years old. The nausea, the loss of time and the despair that migraines bring with them have had a huge, often overwhelming impact on my life. They also brought a mistrust of myself; I never knew when they would appear and strike me down, so I couldn't count on myself to function. I envied people who never got them.

They brought addiction too. Prescription painkillers through to opiates, I have tried them all. When morphine and pethidine stopped working, I was forced to go cold turkey and stop taking everything. I found out years later that what I had been battling was analgesic rebound, where taking the meds eventually brings on another more severe headache and so it goes on and on.

I now take nothing, not even paracetamol, so terrified am I of this cycle of dependency. I'm working on other, more positive coping strategies.

Migraine

You came two days ago
In stockinged feet
Assuring me you wouldn't hurt me
Masquerading as a stuffy nose
Unease, agitation and malaise
You fooled me
Again

Yesterday you grew
Ever so slowly
Until your stockinged feet became
Hard leather boots
Kicking my stomach
Stomping on my eyes
Smashing my skull
Again

You are too clever for me
I fall for you every time
You are good at your job
You alone can stop me in my tracks
I retreat to the darkness
I give in
Again

All is pain, nausea and fear
Inside the prison of my head
On and on
Hour after hour
Sleep, total dark and time
Are my only weapons against you
My curse.

> I must learn to stop myself
> Without you
> I know I have the strength
> But today I am wasted
> You have wasted so much of my life
> This has to stop
> Today

I am trying to realise that I am strong enough to give the migraines up, to take responsibility for the way I feel and to relax and give my brain and body a rest. I practise mindfulness meditation daily. It has allowed me to banish yet another ghost from my past.

I'm sure I dream frequently but I rarely remember my dreams, so I do not have a dramatic, terrifying or even picturesque dream life as many people do. Nevertheless, I have had several dreams with a recurrent theme.

In the most recent, I am in my car with one of my young children. I am a long way from home, way out in the country, in a tunnel, an abandoned factory or some other undesirable place. I am lost. I don't know how to get out. I am never rescued nor do I ever solve my distressing dilemma by myself. Consequently, I wake in a highly anxious state.

I am reminded of a real-life panic attack I experienced some years ago. I was driving my car with my very young daughter in the back seat when the attack came on. As I was on a freeway, I had to maintain a high speed and couldn't pull over to the side. I felt trapped. I had to keep going at all costs. I was terrified. I believed I was going to lose control of the car, that it would leave the freeway at speed and we would crash. I was convinced I was going to die, or be in the most terrible accident, where my leg would become trapped and subsequently amputated. They were the only two outcomes, death or amputation, nothing less. I gripped the steering wheel tightly to try to keep the car on course as my knuckles turned white. My breathing became shallow; it was like a nightmare that went on forever. Finally, I got to the end of the freeway onto a regular two-lane road and

I started to relax, breathe and soften my grip on the wheel. Overcome with emotion, I cried and yawned and yawned.

I have not driven on a freeway since. I still avoid driving especially on unfamiliar roads, in traffic, at speed, over bridges, through tunnels, out in the country or at night. There is a pattern here. Alone and responsible, vulnerable, trapped, frightened of what could happen, scared of possible pain, disaster, loss of control. Is this not the same as what I see in my dreams?

I have not always been like this. I used to love driving anywhere under any conditions. What caused the change?

I recall a traumatic event, much more recent.

'Your calf muscle could detach. Your tendon has a hole in it and could snap at any time.'

The words sounded so reasonable, so logical, I felt no desire to question them.

'We can cut away the hole and then sew up the tendon so it's strong again.'

Of course you can, that sounds quite simple and straightforward, I thought. As well as having film star looks, you are the best orthopaedic surgeon in the city. Easy, then I can go back to the gym. That, after all, was my main motivator, and probably the main cause, of the presenting problem.

I was a gym junkie, a would-be bodybuilder. Strength, muscle size and body image were everything. I had experienced many unwelcome training-related injuries. They impeded my progress and interrupted my rhythm as well as causing me pain, but at that time in my life, pain was secondary. I needed to be strong; I hated the feeling of weakness, vulnerability. And I liked the way I looked. I ask myself now why that was so important to me. Did I equate physical strength with emotional strength?

If my calf muscle became detached, I would not be able to walk, let alone train. The latter scared me more than surgery. I wasn't remembering that life is full of irony.

So, gullible me, blindly gave herself over to the knife. The operation would be quick, I would be fine, it would be a walk in the park. Which is exactly what happened: it was quick and I was back in the recovery room.

'There's something wrong, very wrong,' I was saying to myself.

Even though I must still be under the effect of the anaesthetic, I can feel a most uncomfortable chafing under the back slab of plaster that has been placed on my leg to immobilise it. This post-operative procedure was designed to aid the healing, now there's an irony. I complain to the nurses, who seem unsure, confused, embarrassed? It gets worse. They decide to cut down the ridge of plaster on which my calf muscle was resting. There is some relief but it still hurts.

The handsome 'best in the city' surgeon is called in. 'It appears there has been some accident.'

I see it as an almighty stuff-up. No one is claiming responsibility. They are all scratching their heads, stroking their invisible beards. Meanwhile, I am released from hospital, with crutches and dressings. I return to work, crutches and plaster come off but the sore on the back of my calf remains. My troublesome ankle, the original problem, is cured and healed. I have to visit the surgeon regularly to get the dressing changed. I come to loathe his George Clooney looks. Is he a real surgeon or merely a good-looking actor, I wonder.

One day, Doctor Clooney, while changing the dressing says, 'Oh, there are black spots on the wound. You must go to hospital immediately. You have gangrene.'

WHAT? I can't believe it. Gangrene, that's World War I stuff, that's trenches, getting blown up, being carted on a stretcher to a field hospital where nurses in white starched uniforms tend to men whose limbs have become putrid with rot and have to be AMPUTATED. I am appalled, horrified, scared I could die. Doctor Clooney has become Doctor Death.

I am quickly despatched to a nearby hospital, where I and my gangrene are taken to be repaired by a plastic surgeon. I think to myself, those poor wide-eyed World War I soldiers did not have this luxury. Nonetheless, I am still terrified and the pain has become intense. I want the poison out now.

The plastic surgeon, who is indeed a god, attempts to explain to me through my morphine fog that he has to cut out the gangrenous part of my leg and also slice a thin piece of skin from somewhere else on my body to cover the hole left behind. This macabre procedure is called a skin graft. He is honest and tells me that sometimes skin grafts have to be done again and again before they are successful. I literally don't care what he does as long as he takes away the searing pain deep in my calf. The operation is scheduled straight away; time is critical.

I have many World War I thoughts.

I wake up in recovery to find the pain in my calf has been replaced by a sharp stinging sensation like when you fall off your bike and graze your leg badly on the asphalt. Only this stinging is coming from high up on the outer side of my thigh. I discover it is the donor site from which Doctor Wonderful has created the top piece of pastry for the lid of the pie. At least he has taken it from the same leg, so I will have one unscarred leg. I feel so much better but very shell-shocked, possibly like those poor World War I soldiers.

All went well; now I just had to hope that the graft would heal.

Then something strange happens. A friend of mine comes in to visit. She says she would like to perform reiki on me to assist the healing.

I say, still a little drug-fuzzy, 'Sure. Knock yourself out.'

I am not a believer, more agnostic about reiki. In fact, all I know is that it allegedly involves a transfer of energy from the practitioner to the patient. I am sceptical but beyond caring at this stage.

She begins. She does not touch my leg, merely holds her hands some distance above the wound. To my utter disbelief, I feel instant warmth, almost heat, in the damaged areas of my leg. Reason shouts at me, this can't be happening, but it is; each time my friend holds her hands over the wounds, I experience a flood of warmth which only ceases when she ends the session.

I have never before or since had such an experience – pleasant, but rather creepy. I like to be able to explain events but this seemed inexplicable at least in a scientific way. Nonetheless, my skin graft healed beautifully, requiring no further attention. I learnt that day that there are some things in life that are impossible to explain, that life is indeed a mystery and that there is much that we do not understand.

I was left with two sizeable scars. One was more like a crater that had been dug out of the flesh on my calf. Fortunately, the brilliant plastic surgeon had removed all the dead flesh down to the muscle.

When I returned to work, I referred to my scarred leg as the result of a shark bite. The kids in my classes loved it and would plead with me, 'Tell us your shark story, Miss.' I think many of them believed my shark tale, as everyone knows that all that comes out of a teacher's mouth is God's honest truth.

The real truth was that I found the crater disgusting. I felt disfigured, undesirable and ugly. I refused to wear dresses, skirts or shorts. My calf looked and felt to me like a hollowed-out meat pie that had been covered crudely with pale, lumpy pastry. It certainly put a sizeable dent in my self-image. Sleek, strong Wonder Woman now had a flaw. I felt vulnerable, terrified of something banging into my leg, like a supermarket trolley. I returned to the gym but I think something more than my calf had been dented.

I realise now that I indeed had a form of shell shock or PTSD, as it is called now. Fear of further trauma is what the psychologist told me when I ended up in treatment for panic attacks some time later. The attacks always involved a terror of losing my legs in an imagined car accident. Were they linked to my dreams?

12
The Other M Word

Two M words have shaped my life, both neurological conditions. One I have already spoken about is migraine and the other is MS, multiple sclerosis.

After running my car into a wall for no apparent reason, seeing white spots at the edges of my vision, and being alarmed by an unruly shoulder spasm, I was feeling confused and vulnerable. Suspecting a brain tumour, my GP sent me to a neurologist for further tests. After a string of tests, the diagnosis was that I in fact had MS. I didn't hear another word the doctor said after he uttered those two letters. I was shocked to my core.

My first reaction was wheelchair, disabled, dependent. How would I be able to look after my young daughter? To be told you have a degenerative neurological condition which is potentially life-threatening and for which there is no cure is overwhelming to say the least. My super-fit body was failing me again.

A Testing Time

It began with a twitch
In my right shoulder
That wouldn't
Go away
I drove my car
Into a wall too
That made me worried
My GP, a man I trusted
said
It could be a brain tumour

You need tests
You need to see a neurologist
I became more worried
My neurologist
A kind gentle young man
Sent me off for
The Test Trio
Lumbar puncture
MRI and VEP
Back in his office
I sat shaking
Afraid to know

It's MS

And my world fell apart

I am getting better at recognising them. They are sudden and scary. One type of MS attack occurs when it is hot and or humid, even in an overheated restaurant in the middle of a freezing winter. I become suddenly aware of a feeling of malaise, 'unwellness', an almost out-of-body sensation. I sometimes feel I cannot breathe. I know I must cool myself down. Immediately.

The weird thing is I do not feel hot, I don't sweat, I am not thirsty. This feeling is coming from inside. My legs turn jelly-like, as though the settings on my muscles have been turned to Low but not Off entirely, thank God. My insides also assume this jelly-like state. I seem to wobble inside, like how you feel when you're about to perform on stage. It is terrifying, to feel that you're losing control of your body from within.

Then come the thoughts: what will happen to me, will I faint, collapse or, worse, will I die? Fortunately, I have always been able to bring my core temperature down enough for the attack to pass so I can't report on what would happen, but I confess to being curious.

When I cool down, I become calmer but then my emotions take hold. I become overwhelmed with the urge to cry, then I yawn and yawn and yawn – not polite little yawns, but shuddering, gasping grabs at the air as though I am grateful that I am still able to breathe. All these stages play out like a well-choreographed dance over which I have no control. They are like small panic attacks. Once the yawning stops, which can take some time, I am good to go; I have no residual effects and my strength returns.

MS can suddenly bring a sharp stabbing pain in my eye, like I am being stabbed by a madman with a scalpel, deep into my eyeball. This can last for three or four seconds, then it recedes as my hand flies up to cover my eye, then it is gone. I always fear that my sight will be affected. Luckily it never is; it's just another unsettling reminder that this strange companion, MS, is always with me.

When first diagnosed, I was strongly advised to embark on a treatment program of immunotherapy that I learnt to self-administer with intramuscular injections weekly.

I had never felt so alone, so vulnerable. My daughter was too young to even try to explain this latest challenge to. My other family members and my best friend lived interstate, I had no partner, no significant other to share the challenge and the grief. I had to do it on my own. To add to those layers of difficulty, the treatment was confronting and the side effects disgusting.

So I turned to rituals.

Ritual 1: The Tray

I went to Cheap as Chips and bought the brightest, most colourful, ridiculous tray I could find. I took it home and kept it in a special place in a cupboard. I would bring it out on the assigned day and time and place on it all the paraphernalia that I required to successfully give myself the injections. I would then let my daughter know that I didn't want to be disturbed. It was disturbing enough for me, let alone a little girl, to witness a sharp, long, heavy duty needle penetrating my thigh. Even though I had trained to perform this act correctly by practising on an orange, it rarely was painless. It hurt; sometimes it hurt a lot.

I would then commence. I felt like a junkie, although I reflected that at least a junkie gets some bliss, some reward from her drug; I had no idea if mine was having any effect at all on my MS. All I knew for sure was that it would make me feel terrible after about thirty minutes. I always got bad headaches, felt nauseous and shivery; the inadequately named 'flu-like symptoms'. These feelings would last all the next day. And I had to go to work and function.

After four years of this self-torture, I packed it in. I gave the tray to Goodwill and took no further MS treatment.

Ritual 2: Religion (yes, religion)

I am mildly embarrassed to say at this quite challenging time in my life I turned to another ritual. I decided that, in the absence of a partner, a significant other, I needed Catholicism.

I realise now I just needed a structure, something I felt I could rely on, a framework into which I could place this sudden brush with mortality. I guess I felt it was yet another example of being betrayed, except this time it wasn't being done *to* me, it was being done *by* me. My own central nervous system had betrayed me. It had attacked itself and was threatening to gradually consume me and then spit out, like pips from an orange, mental and physical decline and above all dependence. I was anticipating the grief I felt sure was ahead of me.

So I took myself to Catholic classes and, being the perfectionist that I am, didn't miss one, did all my homework and got myself baptised and confirmed in one fell swoop. I mixed with people I wouldn't have normally even thought of passing the time of day with: nuns, lay ministers, eager parents who hastily had to establish their religious status in order to get their kids baptised and thereby into Catholic schools. The lost, the searchers, the scholars.

I must admit I enjoyed the intellectual rigour of discussing biblical texts; I found it much like being back at uni analysing works of literature. I relish dissecting and rearranging words and sentences to create new meaning. I learnt that many nuns were highly intelligent women, educated, flexible and, above all, feminist, unlike priests. I felt a connection to them, but couldn't relate to the parish community as a whole.

I kept my conversion private, fearing excommunication from my many gay friends. I felt like a fraud. Deep down, I knew I still did not believe in the existence of God. I had come to this realisation early in life and nothing, not even fear of dying, could change that. But I did enjoy the rituals; the Catholics do them so well. I guess my abhorrence of being exposed as a fraud and my love of integrity overcame my need for religious solace.

I now have no need for rituals. Even though this condition is presumed to be degenerative, I try hard to keep it at bay with powerful natural strategies like positive thinking and removing stress and toxic people from my life. I stay fit, active and lean. I also follow a strict vegan diet and I meditate daily, where my aims are peace and insight through mindfulness. I no longer take any medication for MS, just mega-doses of vitamin D three-monthly. I live and play within my limits, and am not too proud to ask for help when I need it. I have learnt to live and even thrive with MS; indeed, it has set me on a new life path.

And it has not progressed.

13
Active Witness

It has taken me a long time to change the focus in my life, to no longer fear the ghosts of my past but to look with confidence to the future. The pain, the loss and the betrayals which followed me to Sydney are retreating from my consciousness. They are no longer just beneath the surface, lurking like ghosts, waiting to overpower me. I am now learning to focus on the wealth of good things in my life and, importantly, on all the positives I have experienced and witnessed in my past as well. There is a balance now; the dark is not shutting out the light.

I had become accustomed to directing all my energies towards the fight, the challenge, readying myself for the struggle, always anticipating darkness. But I now understand that living with that constant flight or fight response is damaging to my physical and mental health. I have learnt that, because my mother wasn't able to model how to be calm, I never learnt it. I had to learn from scratch how to be at peace because it didn't come naturally. I feel a little unsure of this new approach, where anxiety is replaced by calm and acceptance. I feel like I'm dipping my toes into the ocean for the first time, but I like it. I feel lighter, I smile more.

Maybe this is what happens as you get older. Maybe this newfound optimism was there all along just waiting to be unearthed.

These days, former battles have been replaced by a calm but active witness to the world around me. I have discovered that I can be of more help to myself, and those I love, if I stand at a distance, ready to help but not allowing myself to be engulfed by challenges in my life and in theirs. Mindfulness meditation has taught me two things I wish I had learnt years ago: how to accept life and how to tame my empathy. As Matthieu Ricard says, 'Compassion is much more useful in helping others than empathy.'

Before I gained these insights, I felt as if I were a little cup, about to overflow.

This Little Cup

I am a little cup
Into me pours
Constantly
Tasks. Problems that need solving
Dilemmas. Crises that need avoiding
Decisions. Plans. Worries
Responsibilities. Duties
Fears. Terrors and Dread
All mixed in with
The dark shadows of guilt

This little cup
Tries hard to contain the flow
But it is too small
It spills over
There is no bigger cup
Underneath to catch the excess
So it cracks

Pain slithers in
And with it comes
A brutal respite
But the cracks remain
Until the next overflow
I must learn to control the flow
Or this little cup might break

I feel that I have entered yet another life. I have grown from daughter to wife, to mother to ex-wife, to mother-in-law to grandmother. Becoming a grandmother brings a wondrous mix of feelings: joy, concern, fear, warmth but, above all, an overwhelming love in its purest form. Seeing my son cradle his newborn son is such a potent symbol of the way life moves on relentlessly, miraculously. Feeling my grandson snug in my arms transports me back too: my body remembers the sensation, the softness, the shape, the trusting eyes. And then to actually witness my daughter giving birth, being present and assisting in that miracle, was transformative.

My place in the universe seems more tangible now. I can relinquish some of the work, the responsibilities, to others now and soak up the richness of life from an emotionally safe distance.

I look forward to this new role of active witness. I am doing everything in my power to be as healthy as I can in mind and body for as long as I can. I plan to be around long enough to grow old, really old.

Draw back the curtains and enjoy the view.

www.ingramcontent.com/pod-product-compliance
Lightning Source LLC
Chambersburg PA
CBHW030915080526
44589CB00010B/323